History Makers

Modern World Leaders

Neil Morris

 Chrysalis Children's Books

First published in the UK in 2003 by

Chrysalis Children's Books
64 Brewery Road, London N7 9NT

Copyright © Chrysalis Books PLC 2003
Text by Neil Morris°

A Belitha Book

ISBN 1 84138 725 8

British Library Cataloguing in Publication Data for this book is available from the British Library.

Editorial Manager: Joyce Bentley
Assistant Editor: Clare Chambers
Editor: Rosalind Beckman
Designer: Sarah Crouch
Picture Researcher: Jenny Barlow

Printed in Hong Kong
10 9 8 7 6 5 4 3 2 1

Picture credits:

B = bottom; L = left; R = right; T = top.

Cover front and back Rex 4 Reuters/Larry Downing 5 L Rex/Sipa R Reuters/Jeff Christensen 6 and 7 Mary Evans 8 Hulton Archive 9 T Hulton Archive B Mary Evans 10 and 11 Hulton Archive 12 David King Collection 12-13 Rex 13 David King Collection 14 Hulton Archive 15 T Hulton Archive B Mary Evans 16 Hulton Archive 17 T Rex B Hulton Archive 18 Rex/Sipa 19 T Hulton Archive B Rex 20 T Hulton Archive B Corbis/Bettmann 21 Hulton Archive 22 and 23 David King Collection 24 Hulton Archive 25 David King Collection 26 Rex/Sipa 27 T Hulton Archive B Corbis/Bettmann 28 Rex /Sipa 29 T Rex B Rex/Sipa 30 Rex/Sipa 31 T Corbis/Doria Steedman B Rex/Sipa 32 Rex/Sipa 33 T Hulton Archive B Rex/Sipa 34 David King Collection 35 T David King Collection B Hulton Archive 36 Rex/Jeroen Oerlemans 36-37 and 37 Reuters/Rafael Perez 38 Rex/Sipa 39 T Corbis/Michael Nicholson B Rex/Sipa 40 Rex/Prisma/Matteini-Bertolucci 41 T Corbis/Peter Turnley B Reuters/Blake Sell 42 Rex/Sipa 43 T Rex/Sipa B Rex/Richard Oliver 44 Hulton Archive 45 T Reuters/Scanfoto B Reuters/Pool.

All reasonable efforts have been made to trace the relevant copyright holders of the images contained within this book. If we were unable to reach you, please contact Chrysalis Children's Books.

CONTENTS

INTRODUCTION

The world has always had leaders. Most have ruled over people in one particular region or country. Some military commanders such as Alexander the Great and Napoleon tried to build up huge empires. In more recent times, some leaders have become especially important because of their power and influence throughout the world. In this book, we look at the fascinating lives of ten of the world's most important modern leaders.

Presidents Vladamir Putin of Russia and George W. Bush of the United States shake hands. They are two of the world's most powerful leaders.

The twentieth century

At the beginning of the twenty-first century, it is interesting to look back at the leaders who shaped the last 100 years. One of the most important features of the period was that it contained two world wars. These conflicts affected the lives of everyone, including our leaders.

Misuse of power

Not all the leaders in this book were forces for good, but their actions affected people all over the world. Lord Acton, a nineteenth-century British historian, said: 'All power tends to corrupt, and absolute power corrupts absolutely.' Some leaders ruled as brutal **dictators** and misused their power by crushing all their opponents.

Political systems

Just like ordinary people, leaders either have to deal with the world in which they grow up or they want to try and change it. Some major twentieth-century leaders were involved with **communism**. Joseph Stalin helped to enforce communism and widen its influence. Mao Zedong spread it throughout China. Under Mikhail Gorbachev, communism lost its power in Russia and Eastern Europe. Fidel Castro continues the system in Cuba.

Great personalities

Great leaders have strong personalities; often they become popular heroes. Churchill's 'V for victory' sign gave hope to millions of people. Kennedy's youth and good looks made him a popular president throughout the world. Indira Gandhi showed that women can lead as well as men. Ayatollah Khomeini came to represent the **Islamic revolution** for the people of Iran and other **Muslim** countries. Nelson Mandela gave hope to all the world's oppressed people.

In 1988 Benazir Bhutto became the first female leader of a Muslim country.

Kofi Annan, an experienced international administrator from Ghana, became Secretary General of the United Nations in 1997.

United Nations

Though their life stories are not told here, leaders of international organisations also play an important part in the world today. They help bring people together, including political leaders, which can only be good for people's welfare and world peace. The Secretary General of the **United Nations**, as well as those who head the world's relief organisations and international environmental groups, are all important leaders.

ADOLF HITLER

1889-1945

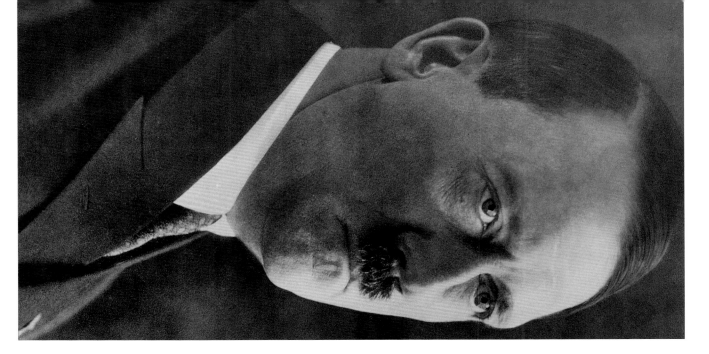

Hitler was the brutal dictator of Nazi Germany. He brought about World War II and was responsible for the deaths of many millions of people worldwide.

Adolf Hitler was born in Braunau, a small town in Austria across the River Inn from Germany. His mother, Klara, was the third wife of a customs official named Alois Hitler, who had been born Schicklgruber. He had later taken the surname of his stepfather, Johann Hiedler, which he then changed to Hitler.

To Linz, Vienna and Munich

When Adolf was six, his parents moved to Linz. There the young Hitler did very poorly at school. His father died in 1903 and four years later he went to Vienna to study art. But he was turned down by the Art Academy and spent his time drifting around the poor districts of the city. He earned little money at this time as he was unable to hold down a job for very long; In 1913 Hitler moved to the Bavarian town of Munich, in Germany. The Austrian Army called him back for a medical examination but they said he was unfit for military service.

Adolf Hitler abused his power as a leader. His policies spread death and destruction throughout the world.

In prison

In 1924 Hitler spent nine months in Landsberg prison. There he wrote the first part of his book *Mein Kampf* ('My Struggle'). In it he stated that Germans were superior to any other people, and he expressed great hatred of all other nations. He accused Jewish people of ruining Germany, which he said was destined to rule the world. He took the opportunity to say that Germans needed to unite behind a great Führer (or 'leader') – Hitler himself.

German corporal

When World War I broke out in 1914, Hitler joined the German Army and became a messenger, crossing battlefields under fire, for which he was awarded the Iron Cross for bravery. He became a corporal and was in hospital suffering from the effects of poison gas when Germany surrendered in 1918.

National Socialist Party

Back in Munich, Hitler joined a small political group and helped build it up into the National Socialist German Workers' Party (called Nazi Party for short). He gained support with speeches about bringing jobs and wealth back to Germany. He set up an army of brown-shirted soldiers, called **stormtroopers**, and in 1923 they helped him try to take over the Bavarian government. When this failed, Hitler was arrested and sent to prison.

In 1914 Hitler (far right) joined the 16th Bavarian Infantry Regiment.

The Nazis regularly held large rallies like this one in Nuremberg.

The 'Third Empire'

After his release from prison, Hitler built up his party again. At first the Nazis were not taken very seriously, but this changed in 1929, when the **Depression** hit Germany and millions lost their jobs. Hitler led protest marches, held mass meetings and made stirring speeches. In the 1932 elections the Nazis were Germany's strongest party. The following year, President Hindenburg appointed Hitler as Chancellor, head of the German government. Hitler moved quickly to head off any opposition within Germany. His secret police hunted down opponents to the new state, which Hitler called the Third Reich, or 'Third Empire'. (He said the first had been the Holy Roman Empire, and the second the German Empire of 1871-1918.)

Hitler Youth

When Hindenburg died in 1934, Hitler became head of the German State and was able to rule as a dictator. The Nazis used **propaganda** to press home the 'new order' that they wanted to bring to German society. Boys had to join the Hitler Youth organisation, wear its uniform and learn Nazi beliefs. Girls joined the Society of German Maidens and took up gymnastics.

World War II

Hitler played on the weakness of other nations and the divisions between them. In 1938 his troops invaded Austria, and early the following year they took Czechoslovakia. Next on the list was Poland, but when Hitler's troops invaded in 1939, Britain and France declared war on Germany. This was the start of World War II.

The Holocaust

The Holocaust (meaning 'widespread destruction') is the name given to the mass murder of European Jews by the Nazis. First, Jewish people had their rights taken away. Then they were forced to live in special areas called **ghettos** and work as slave labourers. Finally, millions were sent to **concentration camps** such as Auschwitz, where many were killed in gas chambers. By the end of the war, the Nazis had murdered six million Jews.

Success turns to failure

At first Hitler's army was successful and he took over a large part of Europe, including France. But his greatest gamble failed. In 1941 he invaded the **Soviet Union** to gain more 'living space' in the East. When this failed, it weakened the German war effort. Nevertheless, Hitler's forces held out against the **Allies.** By 1944, however, Hitler was in poor health and the war was going disastrously for Germany. But still he refused to give in.

Death in the bunker

In early 1945 Hitler was hiding in a concrete bunker beneath Berlin, the German capital. There he was joined by Eva Braun, a young woman who had been his mistress since he came to power. When Russian troops reached Berlin, Hitler at last accepted that the situation was hopeless. On 29 April Hitler and Eva Braun were married in the bunker. The very next day his wife took poison and Hitler shot himself. Their bodies were burned by one of Hitler's personal guards.

Hitler dining with Joseph Goebbels (1897–1945) (left), who led the Nazi propaganda campaigns.

JOSEPH STALIN

1879-1953

Stalin was a ruthless dictator who held absolute power in the Soviet Union for almost 25 years.

Joseph Stalin was born in Gori, a town in Georgia, which was then part of the Russian empire. His real name was Iosif Dzhugashvili.

An only child

Stalin's father was a shoemaker and his mother was a washerwoman. The first three children of the family died when they were young, so Iosif grew up as an only child. When he was eight, his mother sent him to a church school in Gori. Speaking Georgian at home, he learned Russian at school. In 1894 he earned a scholarship to a **seminary** in Tbilisi, the Georgian capital. There he studied to become an Orthodox Christian priest.

Poverty in Russia

Many people in the Russian Empire were beginning to complain about their new emperor, **Tsar Nicholas II.** Millions of peasants were starving and factory workers were poorly paid, but the Tsar refused to grant them higher wages or better working conditions. Those who spoke out against him were arrested.

Stalin ruled his enormous country by terror. Though he led his people to some industrial success, he was generally hated and feared.

Leon Trotsky

Leon Trotsky (1879–1940) met Lenin in London after escaping from exile in Siberia. After the Russian Revolution of 1917, in which he played a major part, he became the first Soviet head of foreign affairs. After Lenin's death, many Communists expected him to become head of the party. But Stalin proved to be clever and ruthless in the power struggle. He had Trotsky expelled from the party in 1927 and then banished from the Soviet Union. Trotsky went to Mexico, where he was murdered in 1940, probably by one of Stalin's secret agents.

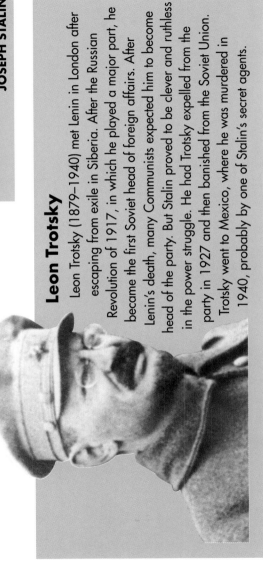

Young revolutionary

Dzhugashvili began reading the works of Karl Marx, a German philosopher who had written about communism, and soon joined a secret Marxist group. In 1899 he was expelled from the seminary for missing an exam; he later claimed he was dismissed for being a **revolutionary**.

Sent to Siberia

Dzhugashvili began organising demonstrations and wrote for Marxist journals. He read articles by the revolutionary Vladimir Ilich Lenin and in 1901 joined the Russian Social Democratic Workers' Party. The following year he was arrested by the secret police and sent to Siberia, in northern Russia. When he escaped, he married Yekaterina Svanidze but in 1907 she died soon after giving birth to their son, Yakov. By then Dzhugashvili had joined Lenin's **Bolsheviks**. Between 1904 and 1912 he spent most of his time in prison or in **exile**, though he escaped on several occasions. In 1913 Dzhugashvili changed his name to Stalin, which means 'man of steel'.

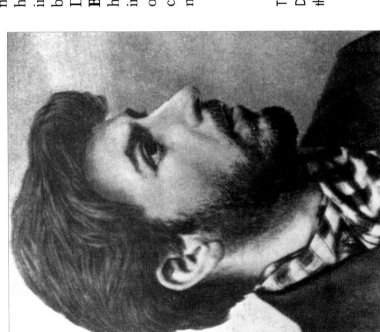

This photograph of Iosif Dzhugashvili (Stalin) was taken by the Russian police around 1902.

This poster from the early 1930s was designed to show young Russians enjoying life on state-owned farms.

The Russian Revolution

Stalin spent the first years of World War I in exile in Siberia. Riots and strikes in Russia led to the Tsar giving up his throne in 1917, and Bolsheviks such as Stalin were released. Lenin and Trotsky led the October Revolution, which gave power to the communists. The Tsar and his family were imprisoned and later shot.

Gaining power

Stalin remarried in 1918 and had a second son, Vasili, and later a daughter, Svetlana. In 1922 he became General Secretary of the Communist Party, which gave him great power in the new Soviet Union. By this time Lenin was ill but he secretly warned his colleagues about allowing Stalin too much power.

Reign of terror

When Lenin died in 1924, the communists ignored his warning and Stalin began taking all the power into his own hands. By 1929 he had got rid of all his rivals, including Trotsky, and was dictator of the Soviet Union. Years before, Stalin had been spied on by the Russian secret police. Now he did exactly the same to others. Millions of Russians who disagreed with his dictatorship were executed or sent to **labour camps** with very harsh conditions. Stalin got rid of anyone who threatened his position.

Germany invades

During the 1930s the Russians were worried about Adolf Hitler's powerful Nazis. In 1939 Stalin suddenly signed an agreement with Hitler that their two countries would not go to war against each other. But in 1941 Hitler went back on his agreement with Stalin and Germany invaded the Soviet Union.

Many people who disagreed with Stalin were sent to labour camps such as this.

The Cold War

The Cold War began after World War II when Stalin tried to increase communism's influence throughout the world. The term was used to describe the hostility between the Soviet Union and its Eastern European allies on the one hand, and the United States and the Western powers on the other. It was called 'cold' because hostilities never turned into open warfare. There were many threats and dangers, but the Cold War finally ended in 1990. This Russian cartoon shows how the Soviets thought Americans were only pretending to want peace.

Military marshal

When the invasion failed, Stalin became more popular in his own country. He named himself Marshal of the Soviet Union and agreed to work with Great Britain and the United States to defeat Germany. But when the war was won in 1945, Stalin set about taking over the countries of Eastern Europe. This led to a long struggle with his former allies.

Removed from honour

By the time Stalin died, in 1953, many Eastern European countries were under communist control. Stalin's body was put next to Lenin in a huge tomb in Red Square, Moscow. Three years later, however, the new Soviet leadership began speaking out against his brutal measures. Then in 1961, Stalin's body was removed from its place of honour and buried in a simple grave.

WINSTON CHURCHILL

1874–1965

Churchill was one of the most popular world statesmen of the twentieth century. His speeches inspired the British people when they were at war with Germany.

Winston Leonard Spencer Churchill was born at Blenheim Palace in Oxfordshire. This magnificent house was built for Churchill's ancestor, the first Duke of Marlborough. Winston's father, Lord Randolph Churchill (1849–95), was a Conservative politician; his American mother, Jennie, was famously beautiful.

School and military academy

The young Winston was sent to a private boarding school but his schoolwork was poor. At the age of 12 he went on to Harrow School, in London, after the headmaster overlooked his blank Latin paper in the entrance examination. When he was 18, Churchill entered the Royal Military Academy at Sandhurst at his third attempt. Once there, he did well in the most important subjects – tactics and fortifications.

As well as being a great statesman, soldier and speaker, Churchill was also a very talented writer and painter.

Writer and painter

Throughout his life Churchill wrote brilliant speeches and informative books. He was awarded the Nobel Prize for Literature in 1953. Some of his best-known books are *World Crisis* (1929), a history of World War I; *Marlborough* (1938), a study of his famous ancestor; and the four-volume *History of the English-Speaking Peoples* (1958). He was also a keen and talented landscape painter. He wrote a book on that subject, too, *Painting as a Pastime* (1949).

Young soldier

In 1895 Churchill joined the 4th **Hussars** Regiment. He served in India and Sudan, and wrote articles on the revolution in Cuba while on leave.

In 1899 he left the army and went to South Africa to cover the **Boer War** as a newspaper reporter. While there, he was captured by the **Boers** and made a daring escape back to British lines.

Churchill as a young war reporter in South Africa.

A career in politics

In 1901 Churchill was elected a Conservative Member of Parliament but disagreements led him to break with his party. He moved to the Liberal Party and in 1908 received his first Cabinet post. In the same year he married Clementine Hozier. Together they had four daughters and a son. In 1911 Churchill was appointed First Lord of the **Admiralty**, in charge of the Royal Navy. Seeing that war would come soon, he set about strengthening the British fleet so that it was well prepared when World War I broke out in 1914.

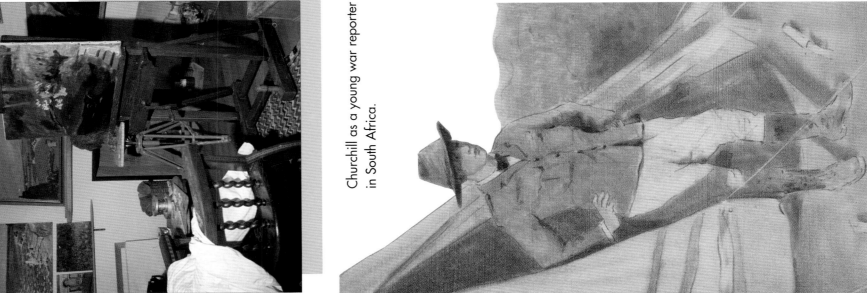

Between the wars

After the war, Churchill continued in government. But three days before the general election campaign began in 1922, he had to have his appendix removed. When he lost the election, he said he was 'without office, without a seat, without a party and without an appendix'. But two years later he rejoined the Conservatives and returned to Parliament. During the 1930s, he opposed those who thought it was better to keep peace with Nazi Germany than risk war. When war finally did break out in 1939, Churchill was again made First Lord of the Admiralty. The British fleet received a simple message: 'Winston is back'.

Prime Minister

In 1940, with the war going badly, the British government fell and Churchill, at the age of 65, became Prime Minister. It was a desperate time but Churchill had the ability to give the British people and their allies confidence. He made memorable speeches. 'We shall not flag or fail,' he told the House of Commons. 'We shall defend our islands whatever the cost may be...we shall fight on the beaches...we shall fight in the hills, we shall never surrender.'

Prime Minister Churchill inspecting bomb damage in Manchester in 1941. He visited many parts of Britain to raise people's spirits.

The famous 'V for victory' sign.

The Battle of Britain

During the war, with bombs falling on London, Churchill ignored air-raid alarms to visit the wounded. He toured military bases, with a large cigar in his mouth and his hand raised in his famous 'V for victory' sign. When British airmen defeated the German air force, Churchill said: 'Never in the field of human conflict was so much owed by so many to so few.'

Prime Minister again

After the war, Churchill's Conservatives lost the 1945 general election to the Labour Party. Then, in 1951, he became Prime Minister again and held the post for another four years. Churchill was knighted by Queen Elizabeth II in 1953. Two years later, he returned to being an ordinary MP, which he remained until 1964, when he finally left the House of Commons. He died a year later, at the age of 90.

The 'Big Three'

Churchill, US President Franklin D. Roosevelt (1882–1945) and Stalin were called the 'Big Three'. The trio first met in November 1943 in Iran, to discuss the British–American invasion of France. In February 1945, they met again to agree on how to occupy Germany when the war was over. Churchill had always been against Communism, and he distrusted Stalin and the Soviet Union. This opposition continued after the war. But Churchill's relationship with America was always good and he was made an honorary US citizen in 1963.

JOHN F. KENNEDY

1917–1963

Kennedy was the youngest man ever elected President of the United States. He was a popular politician, whose death shocked people around the world.

John Fitzgerald Kennedy was born in Brookline, near Boston, into a large, famous family whose ancestors had come from Ireland. His father, Joseph, was a politician and self-made millionaire, whose own father had been a state **senator**. His mother, Rose, also came from a political family – her father had been mayor of Boston. Joseph and Rose had nine children. John (or Jack, as his family called him) was the second eldest.

College sportsman

Kennedy did well at school and was voted the person 'most likely to succeed' by his classmates. In 1935 he went to Princeton University, but after falling ill decided the following year to go to Harvard. While studying politics there, he enjoyed many different sports. He liked swimming and sailing, and was a good footballer. During one American football match he was caught under a pile-up and injured his back, and this gave him problems throughout his life.

John F. Kennedy was the 35th President of the United States, and one of the most popular.

Space race

In 1961 President Kennedy called on the US to 'land a man on the Moon and return him safely to Earth' before the end of the 1960s. This led to the start of the Apollo space program and a race to reach the Moon before the Russians, who sent the first man into space. In 1962, John Glenn (right) became the first American to orbit the Earth. In 1966 the Russians landed an unmanned space ship on the Moon; two years later Apollo 8 flew astronauts around the Moon. Then, on 20 July 1969, Neil Armstrong became the first man to walk on the Moon's surface – JFK's deadline was beaten by just five months.

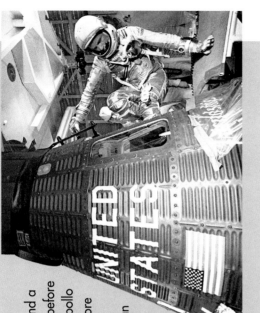

War in the Pacific

In 1943 Kennedy commanded a torpedo boat near the Solomon Islands in the South Pacific. When his boat was cut in two by a Japanese destroyer, he helped his men swim miles to shore.

He spent hours towing one of the wounded crewmen and then went searching for help. The men were rescued five days later, and Kennedy won the Navy and Marine Corps Medal for his courage and leadership.

Jack (second from left) with his parents, brothers and sisters in 1931.

Representative and senator

Kennedy went into politics in 1946, helped in his campaigns by his mother, brothers and sisters. He was elected to the **House of Representatives** as a Democrat, and then in 1952 became a senator. The following year he married Jacqueline Bouvier, a photographic journalist and daughter of a wealthy businessman. After eight years as a senator, Kennedy was ready to run for the highest office in the land.

President

He beat the Republican candidate, Richard Nixon, and was sworn in as president on 20 January 1961. On that day he made the famous statement: 'Fellow Americans, ask not what your country can do for you, ask what you can do for your country.' JFK (as the newspapers often called Kennedy) and his glamorous wife brought informality to the White House. They also brought two young children: Caroline was three and John Jr had just been born.

Mr. and Mrs. Kennedy at Buckingham Palace, London, with Queen Elizabeth II and Prince Philip, in 1961.

The Berlin Wall

In 1961 the East Germans built a wall between East and West Berlin, as the communists tried to stop their citizens fleeing to the West. Kennedy visited Berlin to boost the morale of West Berliners.

Peace Corps

Kennedy set up the Peace Corps in 1961. It is an organisation of volunteers whose aims are to help the poor, promote world peace and increase understanding between America and other nations. The Corps trains men and women for two years of service, when they live and work in another country. Many are teachers; others work in health care or farming. Volunteers must be US citizens and at least 18 years old.

Kennedy signing a treaty banning nuclear testing in 1963, shortly before his death.

Nuclear threat

The following year there was a crisis over Cuba, when Kennedy demanded that the Soviet Union remove nuclear missiles from the island. The US Navy surrounded Cuba and the situation became very dangerous. Finally, Soviet leader Nikita Khrushchev withdrew the missiles and Kennedy agreed not to attack Cuba.

Civil rights

During the early 1960s many black Americans followed Martin Luther King (1929–68) and other leaders in demanding equal rights. Kennedy was against racial discrimination and understood the protesters, but many of his colleagues did not want to upset white voters in the south. Nevertheless, he pressed ahead with a **Civil Rights** **Bill**, saying that 'race has no place in American law or life'.

Death in Dallas

Just after midday on 22 November 1963, Kennedy and his wife were travelling in an open-top car through the Texan city of Dallas. Suddenly, shots rang out and the president was hit in the head and neck. The car raced to the nearest hospital, but it was too late – John F. Kennedy was dead. Shortly afterwards, a man named Lee Harvey Oswald was arrested and charged with murder. Two days later, Oswald was himself shot dead as he was being taken to the county jail. Since then, people have put forward many theories about Kennedy's **assassination**. An official enquiry reported that Oswald acted alone, but others have suggested that there was a secret plot involving others.

MAO ZEDONG

1893–1976

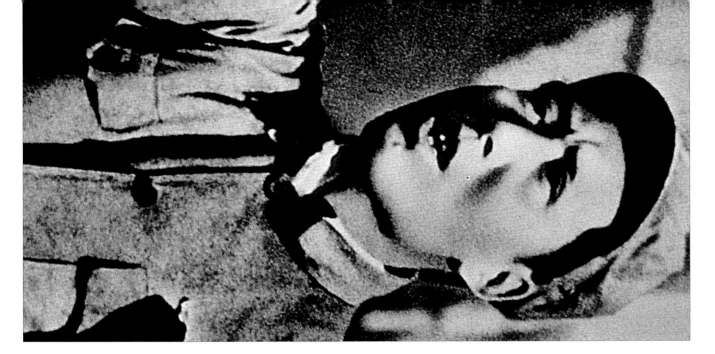

Mao Zedong was a revolutionary leader who helped found the People's Republic of China. He led the world's most populous country for many years.

Mao was born in the village of Shaoshan, in the Hunan province of southern China. His father was a farmer who grew and traded in rice. His mother, who was a devout Buddhist, looked after their modest home and brought up four children. Mao was the eldest, and from the age of seven he worked in his father's fields.

Studies and new influences

At school Mao had to study works by the ancient philosopher Confucius, but he much preferred reading stories about great Chinese warriors and past emperors. He was still a student when a revolution overthrew the Chinese emperor and government in 1911. Mao served in a unit of the revolutionary army for six months, before studying at a teachers' training college in the provincial capital of Changsha. He set up a study group, where fellow students discussed how the new **republic** could be improved.

Mao Zedong (also spelled Mao Tse-tung) was a co-founder of the Chinese Communist Party. This photograph was taken on his famous Long March (see opposite page).

The Long March

When they left Jiangxi in October 1934, the communists were about 100 000 strong. Half were killed during the first three months, as they were bombarded by Nationalist troops. But Mao and the others were determined not to give in. They headed north, crossing 18 mountain ranges and 24 rivers before reaching the north-western province of Shaanxi in October 1935. Only 8000 marchers survived the journey. This heroic, 10 000-km trek inspired many young Chinese to join the Communist Party.

Chinese Communist Party

In 1918 Mao went to work as a library assistant at Beijing University and learned about the ideas and aims of communism. In 1920 he married Yang Kaihui, the daughter of a university professor. The following year, he was one of 12 founding members of the Chinese Communist Party. He lived in Shanghai with his wife and two young sons, and became one of the most important members in the new party. The young communists joined forces with the Nationalist Party (called the Kuomintang) and tried to unite China. But in 1927, the Nationalist leader Chiang Kai-shek (1887–1975) turned on the communists and vowed to wipe out their leaders.

Civil war

In 1927 Mao led hundreds of peasants to the mountains of Jiangxi province, in south-eastern China. The communists formed the Red Army, which fought the nationalists in the countryside. In 1930 Mao's wife was executed by the nationalists; the following year he married He Zizhen, with whom he had five children.

This idealised portrait shows Mao as a young student, full of purpose and ideas.

People's Republic

By 1934 the communists had suffered heavy losses. Mao left his mountain base and headed for the north of the country on his famous Long March. In 1937 Japan invaded China, and the communists and nationalists joined together to fight the common enemy. This uneasy alliance continued throughout World War II, when Mao was forced to spend some of his time living in a cave. Having divorced his second wife, he married a film actress named Jiang Qing. In 1945 he was elected Chairman of the Communist Central Committee, but when the war with Japan ended, trouble broke out again and there was another **civil war**. This time the communists gained great support, until the Nationalists were forced to flee to the island of Taiwan. On 1 October 1949, in Beijing, Chairman Mao announced the birth of the People's Republic of China.

Birthday celebration

In 1949 Mao travelled to Moscow to celebrate Soviet leader Stalin's seventieth birthday. The two communist leaders agreed a treaty of 'friendship, alliance and assistance'.

Jiang Qing (1914–1991) joined the Communist Party at the age of 19. She married Mao in 1939.

Great Leap Forward

At home, the Communist Party and its leader kept a tight grip on people's lives, but in 1956 Mao announced a policy of 'letting a hundred flowers bloom', giving people the freedom to express their own views. Two years later, he started a campaign called the Great Leap Forward. This was supposed to boost the growth of industry by increasing the number of workers and the hours they put in. People had to get together to run small factories in their backyards, but Mao's campaign brought chaos and ended in failure.

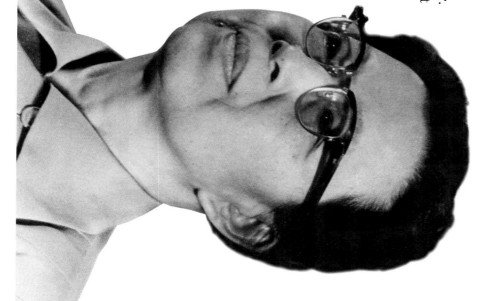

Cultural Revolution

In 1959 Mao stepped down as Chairman of the People's Republic, but he remained head of the Communist Party and kept control of the country. By the early 1960s a split had developed between China and the Soviet Union, and Mao began to feel that his country was losing its way. In 1966 he introduced the so-called Cultural Revolution, led by his wife, Jiang Qing. Universities were closed and many young people joined an organisation called the Red Guards. They attacked party officials who disagreed with Mao. The 'revolution' had become a reign of terror.

Gang of Four

In the late 1960s Mao's health began to fail. He was already ill when he had a historic meeting with US President Nixon in 1972; he died four years later. After his death, his widow joined others in a so-called Gang of Four who tried to seize power. This was unsuccessful and Jiang Qing was put in prison.

This demonstration was held in Beijing in 1968. It was designed to show support for Mao's Cultural Revolution.

The 'Little Red Book'

Throughout his life, Mao wrote many books and articles, as well as poetry. In the early days of the Cultural Revolution, young Red Guards were encouraged to carry a copy of a book called *Quotations from Chairman Mao*. This came to be known throughout the world as the 'Little Red Book'. Along with huge posters and slogans, the book helped turn Mao Zedong into a **cult figure**.

INDIRA GANDHI

1917–1984

Indira Gandhi was the first woman prime minister of India. Both her father before her, and her son after her, were also prime ministers.

Indira Priyadarshini Nehru was born in the northern Indian city of Allahabad, the only child of Jawaharlal Nehru and his wife Kamala. When Indira was little, her father was active in politics. India was then still part of the British Empire. As Nehru supported the movement for Indian independence, he was sent to prison many times. During this period, Indira spent a lot of time at home in her parents' large, comfortable house.

A wide education

Indira was an intelligent, thoughtful child. At the age of just 12 she organised a children's club that supported the Indian independence movement, by helping with chores such as cooking, sewing and first aid. She was sent to many different schools, including a convent in Allahabad and an international school in Switzerland. Her mother died when Indira was 18, and that same year her father sent her to England to study history at Oxford University.

In her two periods as Indian Prime Minister, Indira Gandhi was respected for her strength and qualities as a leader.

Jawaharlal Nehru

Jawaharlal Nehru (1889–1964) was educated in England and went to Cambridge University. He first practised as a lawyer in India, but soon became a follower of Mohandas (known as Mahatma) Gandhi (1869–1948). He agreed with Gandhi's policy of non-violent protest at British rule. After Indian independence, Prime Minister Nehru worked hard to improve living standards for all Indians. Although he was from a wealthy family himself, he did all he could for the nation's poor.

In prison

In 1938 Indira joined the Congress Party; four years later she married a fellow party member, Feroze Gandhi. Though he had the same family name, her husband was not related to the famous Indian independence campaigner, Mohandas Gandhi, who had been a great inspiration to both Indira and her father. Six months after their wedding, Indira and her husband were arrested by the British authorities for their political activities. Mrs Gandhi spent a year in prison, where she taught other inmates to read and write.

Daughter of the nation

When her father became Prime Minister in 1947, Indira acted as his official hostess, helping him to entertain foreign statesmen. She also accompanied him on visits to other countries, and Indian newspapers called her the 'daughter of the nation' and 'India's first lady'. At the same time she became important in the Congress Party, and in 1959 was elected its president. The following year her husband died, leaving her with two teenage sons.

In 1942 Indira Nehru married Feroze Gandhi, a lawyer and politician.

Prime minister

After her father died in 1964, Mrs Gandhi became Minister of Information under the next leader, Lal Bahadur Shastri. When Shastri died two years later, she became Prime Minister of India. She was only the second woman prime minister in the world, following Sirimavo Bandaranaike, who came to power in Sri Lanka six years earlier. In 1971 Mrs Gandhi gained respect for her strength and leadership when Indian troops won a decisive victory over neighbouring Pakistan. This led to the creation of Bangladesh (formerly East Pakistan) as an independent nation.

State of emergency

In 1975 an Indian court announced that Mrs Gandhi had conducted her 1971 election campaign illegally. She refused to resign, however, and responded by declaring a **state of emergency** throughout the country and having her main opponents arrested. In 1977 the people of India voted her out of office, and the following year she and her supporters split from the Congress Party. They formed the new Congress–I Party (the 'I' stood for Indira). After spending two brief spells in prison, Mrs Gandhi was soon back. In 1980 her new party was swept into power and she again became Prime Minister.

Prime Minister Gandhi making a speech. She was known as an effective and confident speaker.

Attack on the Golden Temple

In the early 1980s members of an extreme Sikh religious group used violence in their demands for an independent state of Punjab, in north-west India. Mrs Gandhi thought this threatened Indian unity. In June 1984 she ordered Indian troops to attack armed Sikhs who occupied the Golden Temple at Amritsar, the Sikhs' holiest shrine. More than 450 Sikhs were killed in the battle. This caused great problems between Sikhs and Hindus, who represent the majority religion in India. Five months later, Mrs Gandhi was assassinated in her garden by two Sikh members of her bodyguard. She was succeeded as Prime Minister by her son Rajiv.

The 1984 siege and battle left the Sikhs' Golden Temple in ruins.

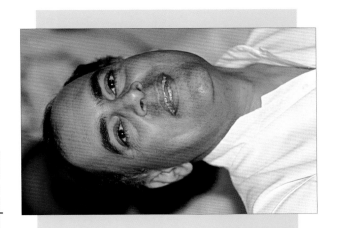

Rajiv Gandhi

Indira Gandhi had two sons, Rajiv (1944–91) and Sanjay (1946–80). Both were educated in India and England. Sanjay went into politics and became his mother's closest adviser. When he was killed in a plane crash, his brother Rajiv took up a political career. He succeeded his mother and was Prime Minister of India from 1984 to 1989. He was respected as a calm politician who always took advice from other members of his party. In 1991 he was assassinated in southern India while campaigning for elections. Seven years later his widow, Sonia Gandhi, was elected leader of the Congress–I Party.

RUHOLLAH KHOMEINI

1900–1989

Ayatollah Ruhollah Khomeini was a religious teacher who led the Islamic revolution in Iran.

Khomeini was born in the town of Khomeyn, in western Iran or Persia as it was then known. His original name was Ruhollah Musawi, but at the age of 30 he took his birthplace as his surname. He was the youngest of the six children of Sayed Musawi and his wife Hajar. Like most Persians, the Musawi family followed the **Shiite** branch of Islam. They were devout Muslims and Ruhollah's father was head of the local religious community.

Islamic studies

When Ruhollah was still a baby, his father was killed on the orders of a local landowner while on a pilgrimage. The boy was brought up by his mother and aunt, and went to a local school. There he learned by heart the teachings of the Koran, the holy book of Islam, as well as reading, writing and arithmetic. His mother died when he was 15, and his oldest brother took on responsibility for him. Four years later he went on to an Islamic college, called a **madrasah,** in the nearby city of Arak.

Ayatollah Khomeini was a respected Muslim scholar and teacher. He returned from exile to lead an Islamic revolution in his homeland of Iran.

Shia Islam

The Islamic religion began almost 1400 years ago when the Prophet Muhammad received revelations from God. There are two major branches of Islam – Sunni and Shia. The vast majority of Iranians are Shiites, who do not accept the first three Sunni successors to Muhammad. They believe that Ali, the fourth successor and Muhammad's cousin and son-in-law, was the true follower of the prophet.

Scholar and teacher

In 1922 Khomeini settled in the city of Qom, where he studied Islamic law. He was also interested in poetry and the ancient Greek philosophers. Five years later he made a pilgrimage to Mecca, in Saudi Arabia, as all Muslims are expected to do. Afterwards, he taught philosophy and law in Qom, building up a great following among his students.

He wrote many articles and books, in which he often criticised the government of Iran.

Religious leader

When the **Shah** of Iran visited Qom in 1953, Khomeini was the only teacher at his college who refused to stand up in respect. He believed that the Shah was destroying Islamic culture. Because of his learning and strong beliefs, Khomeini earned the title **Ayatollah** (an Arabic word meaning 'sign of God'). This title is given only to the most important religious teachers. By the 1960s Khomeini was seen as leader of the whole religious community in Iran.

Iranian supporters carrying posters of the Ayatollah during a demonstration.

Into exile

In 1963 Ayatollah Khomeini criticised reforms brought in by the Shah, including rights for women. He said that changes in traditional law exploited women rather than liberating them. He spoke out so strongly that he was arrested and put in prison. A year later he was exiled to Turkey. He then settled in An-Najaf, Iraq, which is a holy city to Shiites. There he ran a religious school and sent tape-recorded lectures to Iran, where they were played secretly in **mosques.** In 1977 his oldest son Mustafa died mysteriously in An-Najaf. Some people believe he was assassinated by the Shah's security force.

Islamic revolution

In 1978 Iraq's leader, Saddam Hussein, forced Khomeini to leave. He went to Paris, where he was able to follow events in Iran. By then there was massive unrest in his home country, and people were calling for his return. Rioting in the cities led to the Shah leaving Iran in 1979, and just 16 days later Khomeini arrived in the capital, Tehran. Cheering millions lined the streets to welcome him. He took control and the Iranian people voted to make their country an Islamic republic.

Wherever the Ayatollah went in Iran, the faithful reached out to touch him.

Shah of Iran

In 1925 a revolt in Persia led to an army officer, Reza, being made Shah (Persian for 'king'). Ten years later the country's name was changed to Iran. Reza was succeeded by his son, Mohammed Reza Pahlavi (1918–80), who ruled as Shah of Iran from 1941. Strict Muslims thought his policies were too much like those of Western, non-Islamic countries. After the Shah fled Iran for the US, Iranian revolutionaries seized the US embassy in Tehran and took **hostages**, demanding that the Shah be put on trial. This did not happen, but the Shah died in 1980. The hostages were released six months later.

Strict laws

Khomeini and his government ruled the country by strict Islamic laws and tried to prevent all Western, non-Islamic influences. Women were forced to wear traditional chadors – black cloaks that cover the head and drape to the ground. Mixed schools and swimming baths were closed. Western films and television shows were banned, along with Western music, which Khomeini said dulled people's brains. All alcoholic drinks were forbidden. Leaders called on all Muslims to rise up against non-Islamic influences.

Long war

In 1980 Iraqi forces invaded Iran to claim disputed border territories. Iran fought back and a bitter war lasted for eight years. Both sides suffered heavy casualties; Khomeini and Saddam Hussein finally agreed to a ceasefire in 1988. Ayatollah Khomeini continued to keep a tight grip on his country until his death, in 1989. More than a million people attended his funeral, and he was mourned throughout Iran.

Iranian women in grief and mourning at the death of Ayatollah Khomeini.

FIDEL CASTRO

1926–

Castro has ruled Cuba since 1959, when he led a communist revolution that overthrew the previous dictatorship.

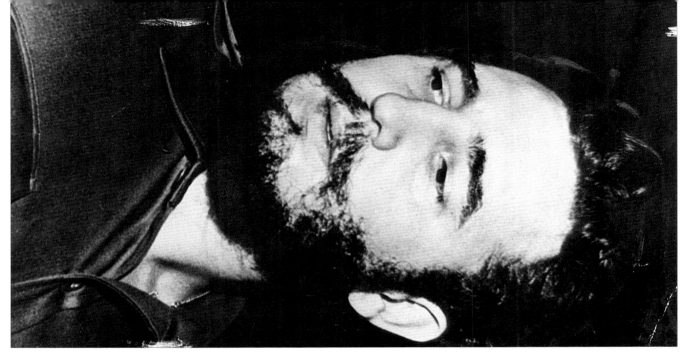

Fidel Castro Ruz was born near Birán, in eastern Cuba, the fourth of seven children. He worked in his father's sugar-cane fields until the age of seven, when he was sent to a Roman Catholic boarding school in Santiago de Cuba. Moving on to high school in Havana, capital of Cuba, he did well in Spanish, history and agricultural studies.

Law and politics

In 1945 Castro went to the University of Havana to study law. While there, he became active in politics. First, he was president of the Students' Federation, then he took part in a failed attempt to overthrow the dictator of the Dominican Republic. He married Mirta Diaz-Bilart (whom he later divorced) and had a son, Fidel. After graduating at the university, Castro became a lawyer in Havana. In 1952 he wanted to stand for election to the Cuban House of Representatives, but elections were cancelled when Fulgencio Batista (1901–73) overthrew the government and took power. Castro was bitterly opposed to Batista.

Fidel Castro has remained in power in Cuba despite opposition from the United States and the collapse of Communism in Russia and Eastern Europe.

Che Guevara

Ernesto Guevara (1928–67), known as Che, was born in Argentina. In 1954 he held a post in the government of Guatemala and the following year went to Mexico. There he met Fidel Castro and joined his revolutionary movement. He became one of Castro's chief commanders and was later made Minister of Industry. In 1965 he left Cuba to lead a rebel group in South America and was killed while trying to overthrow the Bolivian government. During the 1960s Che became a cult hero among students around the world.

26th of July Movement

In 1953 Castro led 160 men in an attack on one of Batista's army barracks. Most of his men were killed, and Castro and his younger brother Raúl were sent to prison. When they were released two years later, they went to Mexico and formed a revolutionary group called the 26th of July Movement (after the date of their first attack).

Failed attack

In 1956 a force of just 80 men sailed from Mexico to Cuba, but when they landed all but 12 were killed. Castro and the other survivors fled to the nearby mountains, where they found wide support from other young Cubans.

Castro and friends, just days after their successful revolution of 1959.

Revolution

By the beginning of 1959 Castro's rebel army had built up to about 800 men. Despite being outnumbered by Batista's professional army, the rebels were so successful that they gained more support among ordinary people in the cities. Realising that he was facing defeat, Batista fled the country. Castro's forces marched triumphantly into Havana. The revolution was complete and Castro became Prime Minister of Cuba.

Difficulties with the USA

In 1960 Castro's government seized American property in Cuba. Castro also signed an agreement with the Soviet Union, which helped the sale of Cuban sugar and the purchase of Russian oil. This led the USA to reduce its sugar imports from Cuba and to break off diplomatic relations. In 1961 the US government encouraged Cuban exiles to overthrow Castro, but this failed. The following year, President Kennedy demanded that the Soviet Union remove its missiles from Cuba (see page 21).

Castro (right) and Mikhail Gorbachev wave to crowds during the Russian leader's visit to Cuba in 1989.

Cuban music

Castro enjoys listening to music, reading books and watching baseball. Cuban music has strong Spanish and African roots. Many dance styles, such as the rumba, conga and cha-cha, either began or were developed in Cuba. In recent years, as music from around the world has become more popular, Afro-Cuban jazz and other styles have made an impact. Groups of singers and musicians such as the Buena Vista Social Club and the Afro-Cuban All Stars have had hits with their albums, and films have been made about their work.

Collapse of the Soviet Union

The USA had always refused to trade with communist Cuba and life became more difficult for Castro as the Soviet Union weakened towards the end of the 1980s. But Castro told his people that Cuba would remain a communist country. Nevertheless, there have been some reforms, such as allowing small businesses to be run privately. In 2000 Russian President Putin visited Cuba and suggested that the two countries might co-operate again in the future. Two years later President Bush confirmed that the US trade **embargo** would remain in force.

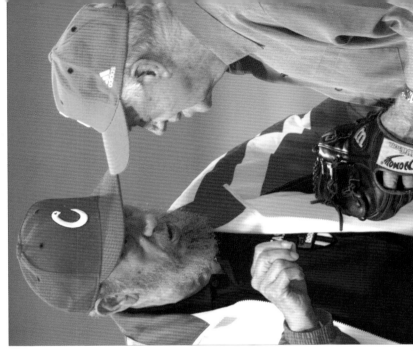

Castro talks baseball with former US President Jimmy Carter.

Economic problems

Castro's government provided better education and health services for its people but the country was dependent on the Soviet Union for economic help. Castro tried to make Cuban farming and industry more efficient but without great success. In 1976 he became President of the State Council, as well as First Secretary of the Communist Party of Cuba. Raúl Castro was made his deputy.

MIKHAIL GORBACHEV

1931–

Gorbachev was leader of the Soviet Union during the last six years of its existence, from 1985 to 1991.

Mikhail Sergeyevich Gorbachev was born in the village of Privolnoye, near the city of Stavropol in southern Russia. His parents, Sergei and Maria, were farmers. Mikhail went to the local village school before going to secondary school in a nearby town. During World War II, his father was called up to the army; Mikhail was eleven when the German army occupied their region in 1942. By the age of 14, he could already drive a combine harvester. From 1946 he spent the summer months helping out at a **collective farm** near his home.

At Moscow State University

At school Gorbachev learned all about the Soviet Union and its leader, Joseph Stalin. In 1946 he joined the Young Communist League, and he did well both there and at school. This made it possible for him to go to university and in 1950 he made the long train journey north to the Russian capital, Moscow. He was not sure what he wanted to study at Moscow State University but he finally chose law.

Mikhail Gorbachev's foreign policies helped bring an end to the Cold War.

Glasnost

Gorbachev introduced *glasnost* ('openness') in order to encourage new ideas. This policy meant that more freedom was given to the press and ordinary people were allowed to speak their minds. There was less **censorship** and people could also follow their chosen religion. Some of those who had been imprisoned for working against the state were released. These changes reduced the power of the central government in Moscow's Kremlin (shown right).

Party work

While he was at university, Gorbachev became a full member of the Communist Party. He also met a philosophy student named Raisa Titorenko, and the two students married in 1954. Gorbachev decided he did not want to become a lawyer. After university he and Raisa went to Stavropol, where he worked for the local Young Communist League. In 1959 they had a daughter, Irina. Gorbachev ran the agricultural department for the region, while he received a diploma in the economics of farming from the local agricultural institute.

Mikhail Gorbachev at the age of 14. The year 1945 meant a great deal to the young man. His father Sergei returned from the war, and when he wasn't busy with schoolwork, Mikhail helped him on the collective farm.

To the very top

By 1970 Gorbachev had risen to become first secretary of the regional party committee. His success was noticed in Moscow, and in 1971 he became a member of the powerful central committee of the Communist Party. He returned to Moscow in 1978, when the Communist Party put him in charge of agriculture. The farmer's son was now responsible for decisions that affected all farming families throughout the Soviet Union. This was a difficult job but, despite some poor harvests, Gorbachev did it well enough to become a member of the **Politburo** – the committee responsible for all Soviet policies.

Raisa Gorbachev accompanied her husband on many of his trips abroad.

New policies

After three general secretaries died between 1982 and 1985 – Leonid Brezhnev, Yuri Andropov and Konstantin Chernenko – Gorbachev found himself head of the party. Though he was still the youngest member of the Politburo, he was now the most powerful man in the Soviet Union. Gorbachev used his power to bring in new policies of *glasnost* ('openness') and *perestroika* ('restructuring'). These aimed to make Soviet society freer and more flexible, but they were not popular with many old-fashioned Communists. The new leader also worked towards reducing the risk of nuclear war. In 1987 he agreed with US President Reagan to destroy stocks of certain types of nuclear missiles.

Reform in Eastern Europe

In 1989 many Communist countries in eastern Europe – the so-called Soviet bloc – wanted to change their system. People rebelled against their rulers and fought for free elections. Unlike all previous Soviet leaders, Gorbachev allowed non-Communist governments to come to power in such countries as East Germany, Poland and Czechoslovakia. He then withdrew Soviet troops from these regions. The Berlin Wall (see page 20) was pulled down in November 1989, and the following year East and West Germany reunited as a single nation. In 1990 Gorbachev was awarded the Nobel Peace Prize for his reforms.

Russian Federation

After the break-up of the Soviet Union, the new Russian Federation came into being. It was by far the largest Soviet republic and the Russian Federation remains the largest country in the world, with Moscow as its capital. The flag that flew over the Russian Empire from 1699 to 1918 was brought back in 1991. The first President, Boris Yeltsin (1931–), ruled until 2000; Vladimir Putin (1952–) succeeded him.

New interests

In 1992, Gorbachev became head of a research group called the International Foundation for Socio-Economic and Political Studies. The following year he was founding president of Green Cross International, an organisation that works to protect the environment around the world. His wife, Raisa, died in 1999.

Former US President Ronald Reagan driving Gorbachev around his ranch. The two men signed an arms limitation treaty for their countries in 1987.

Break-up of the Soviet Union

In 1990 Gorbachev was elected to the new post of President of the Soviet Union. But his reforms had also encouraged freedom movements within many of the 15 republics that made up the Union. Many republics demanded freedom from Soviet control, while others said that their own regional governments were more important than the Politburo in Moscow. Traditionalists in the Communist Party wanted their President to take a tougher line with the republics, and they tried to overthrow Gorbachev. He and his family were arrested while on holiday but the **coup** failed when the President of the Russian Republic, Boris Yeltsin, opposed it.

End of the presidency

Gorbachev remained Soviet President, but the separate republics were working towards a new, looser federation. The power was now with them, and especially the Russian republic. On 25 December 1991 Gorbachev resigned as President and the Soviet Union ceased to exist.

NELSON MANDELA

1918–

After spending more than 27 years in a South African prison, Nelson Mandela became his country's first black president.

Nelson Rolihlahla Mandela was born in the village of Mvezo, in the South African region of Transkei. His family belonged to the Tembu people and his father was chief of the village. His mother was the chief's fourth wife, and altogether his father had four sons and nine daughters. When he was very young, Nelson moved with his mother to the nearby village of Qunu. After his father died, when Mandela was nine, he was brought up by another Tembu chief, who acted as his guardian.

Training in law

In 1938 Mandela went to the University College of Fort Hare. After being suspended for organising a student strike, he went to Johannesburg, where he took a job as a clerk in a law firm. In the evenings he worked for a law degree from the University of South Africa. At this time he came into contact with members of the African National Congress (ANC), an organisation that had been fighting for equal rights for black Africans since 1912. Mandela joined the ANC in 1944 and helped set up its Youth League.

Nelson Mandela's long fight against **aparlheid** ended in success.

With the ANC

Black people had no vote in South Africa. When the white government brought in the system of apartheid in 1948, the ANC fought against it on their members' behalf. In 1950 Mandela was elected to the main committee of the ANC. Two years later he and his friend Oliver Tambo (1917–93) opened their own law practice in Johannesburg. In 1956 the government charged Mandela with **treason**, saying that he and the ANC wanted to bring in a Communist government. The trial lasted for five years. In 1958 Mandela married Winnie Madikizela. This was his second marriage – he had married Evelyn Mase 12 years earlier, but they were divorced.

Under apartheid, all black Africans had to carry a special pass at all times. In protest, Nelson Mandela joined others in burning his pass.

Fighting apartheid

Apartheid (an Afrikaans word meaning 'separateness') was a system of racial **segregation**. It was introduced by the ruling National Party in 1948. The system classified all South Africans into four racial groups: white, black, coloured (mixed race) and Asian. There was segregation in housing, education, transport and places such as lavatories and beaches. The non-white groups were restricted from even entering white neighbourhoods. The ANC bitterly opposed apartheid, and they were supported by people from all over the world.

Sent to prison

In 1960 tragedy struck the South African **township** of Sharpeville, when the police killed 69 black demonstrators. The government enforced their policy by declaring the ANC illegal, which meant they could only continue as an underground movement. Mandela helped form a new, armed branch called Umkhonto we Sizwe ('Spear of the Nation'). He secretly visited many other African countries, but in 1962 he was captured and charged with leaving the country illegally. He was sentenced to five years in prison. In 1963, police found arms and equipment at the Spear of the Nation headquarters. Mandela and other ANC members were found guilty of **sabotage** and sentenced to life imprisonment.

On Robben Island

Mandela was sent to Robben Island, a maximum security prison on a small island 7 km off the coast near Cape Town. Life there was very hard and, though his wife Winnie and many others worked to free him, his situation seemed hopeless. After 12 years on Robben Island, the government offered him freedom on condition that he agreed to retire to the black **homeland** of Transkei. Mandela realised they were trying to show that he accepted apartheid. He refused the offer.

Free at last

In 1985 Mandela was moved to a different prison near Cape Town. By then people all over the world saw his imprisonment as a symbol of apartheid.

The situation improved when F. W. de Klerk (1936–) became president in 1989. Before long, he lifted the ban on the ANC, and on 11 February 1990 millions watched on television as Nelson Mandela was released from prison. At the age of 71, he was free to start a new life.

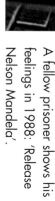

A fellow prisoner shows his feelings in 1988: 'Release Nelson Mandela'.

Joint Nobel Peace Prize

In 1993 Nelson Mandela and President F. W. de Klerk were jointly awarded the Nobel Peace Prize. The two leaders were praised for their 'great political courage'. Although they accepted their prize gracefully, neither said much about the award. They seemed to feel that what they did was necessary rather than admirable. After the 1994 elections, de Klerk became Deputy President, but three years later he resigned as leader of the National Party.

President and head of state

In 1991 Mandela was elected president of the ANC, and in the same year the South African government officially ended apartheid. In April 1994 South Africa's general election was special – it was the first in which people of all races could vote. Mandela led the ANC to victory and became president. During his five-year term of office, he helped improve the quality of houses, schools and hospitals for ordinary South Africans. He also travelled widely and improved his country's relations with its international partners.

Retirement

In 1996 Mandela divorced Winnie and two years later married Graca Machel, the widow of a Mozambican freedom fighter. He announced that he would not stand for re-election in 1999. Instead, he helped his successor as ANC leader, Thabo Mbeki (1942–), win the election and take over the presidency. Mandela has remained a great statesman – people all over the world listen to his opinions on international affairs.

US President Bill Clinton and his wife Hillary visit Mandela's former cell on Robben Island. Mandela was accompanied by Graca Machel.

GLOSSARY

Admiralty The British government department in charge of the Royal Navy.

Allies Countries that join together to fight another. In World Wars I and II, the Allies were the countries fighting with Britain against Germany.

Apartheid System of separating races as practised in South Africa from 1948 to 1991.

Assassination Murder for political reasons.

Ayatollah An important religious teacher and leader in Iran.

Boer War One of two wars between Britain and the Boers (1880–1902)

Boers South African settlers of Dutch descent.

Bolsheviks Russian Communist group.

Censorship Controlling the flow of information, for example, by taking over newspapers, and banning books and films.

Civil rights The rights of every citizen of a country to be free and treated fairly.

Civil war War within a country.

Collective farm Large state-owned farm worked by many different farmers.

Communism Political system in which all property and industry are owned and controlled by the state rather than by individuals.

Concentration camp A place where large numbers of political prisoners are held and often mistreated.

Coup A sudden revolt to overthrow the government of a country.

Cult figure A person who is excessively respected and praised.

Depression Collapse in industry and business, leading to a loss of jobs.

Dictator Ruler with uncontrolled power and authority.

Embargo Ban on trading with a particular country.

Exile Being sent away from one's homeland.

Ghetto Part of a city where a minority group lives.

Homeland Region where black South Africans had to live under apartheid.

Hostage Person seized and held until demands are met.

House of Representatives The lower house of the US Congress that passes laws.

Hussars Soldiers who fight on horseback.

Islamic Concerned with the religion of Islam followed by Muslims.

Labour camp Prison camp where inmates are forced to do hard work and conditions are poor.

Madrasah College for Islamic instruction.

Mosque Muslim place of worship.

Muslim Follower of the religion of Islam.

Politburo Committee responsible for making policies in the former Soviet Union.

Propaganda A programme of publicity, information and misinformation used to further a cause.

Republic State governed by the people or their elected representatives.

Revolution Forcible, usually violent, overthrow of a government to set up a new one.

Revolutionary Person involved in revolution.

Sabotage Deliberate acts of damage and destruction.

Segregation Separation (of races).

Seminary A training college for priests.

Senator Elected member of the Senate (upper house of the US Congress).

Shah Former king of Iran (Persia)

Shiite Follower of the Shia branch of Islam (the other branch is Sunni).

Soviet Union Union of 15 communist republics (from 1922 to 1991), of which Russia was the largest and most powerful.

State of emergency Time when a government says there is danger and a need for special laws.

Stormtroopers Political soldiers who worked for the German Nazi Party.

Township Town or suburb where black South Africans had to live under apartheid.

Treason Betrayal of a country by trying to overthrow its government.

Tsar Former emperor of Russia.

United Nations International organisation of countries set up in 1945 to help world peace and co-operation.

INDEX